T0067370

Nothing Like Christine

Carolyn Townes-Richards

Illustrations by Diane Lucas
Layout, digital images, and editing by Tracy D. Montgomery
Copyediting and proofreading by Maria Fernandes-Jaeger

Living Through Literature with
Aunt CURLY'S Collection

Order this book online at www.trafford.com
or email orders@trafford.com

Most Trafford titles are also available at major online book retailers.

Print information available on the last page.

ISBN: 978-1-4251-1129-8 (sc)

Trafford rev. 06/19/2023

www.trafford.com

North America & international
toll-free: 844-688-6899 (USA & Canada)
fax: 812 355 4082

Dedicated to the life of

Christine Townes-Taylor

Christine was my big sister. She was my "bestest" best friend sometimes, my pretty-good friend at times, and a just-all-right friend when we had two very different views on a given matter. Through all of those times, I loved her and she made a great difference in my life. Believe it or not, we were both born on September 3rd! This was most unusual since we were not twins. I was born five years later. We were two sisters as different as they came; we looked nothing alike. She was short, petite, and a brilliant homemaker who loved to read. "Tene," as she was affectionately called, was talented in arts and crafts, sewing, knitting, and cooking. However, for all the things that were different and unique in our lives. . .we were sisters who had always shared so much. We had a strong love for God and family.

Enjoy this poetic, true life journey about a sister so dear. She was the greatest! Her greatness was in her service—not just service to her family but to everyone she encountered. She's really not gone; just not seen. In my heart and my thoughts, our love will always be remembered as something very special: gentle, joyful, strong, and giving. We shared one of the most wonderful blessings: the incredible and precious gift of being "sisters."

Always remember:

Every good and
perfect gift
comes from God!

Mom's
Baby
Album
For My Firstborn
Christine
September 3rd

Mama's first child was a
cute little girl.
She loved her more than
anything in the world.

She was really tiny,
with eyes big and round.

You'd never believe
she weighed only
three pounds.

Annie Mae
Pricilla Doris
Lillian Mildred
Nyoka Shirley
Barbara Connie
Fahtimah Bea
Jewell Mel
Debora Lillie
Christine Carrie
Annette Cassie
Ethel Sofia
Naomi Ella
Jamie Trin
Tabby Brea

Before she was born,
Mom gathered names.

Her darling little
"queen" she named
"Christine."

Baby
Christine
It's
a Girl!

Hugs and kisses
for her bundle of joy.

A surprise to her
friends, who had
expected a boy.

Mom was so happy. It was all like a dream—that she'd given life to little Christine.

There stood Dad as
proud as could be. He
was telling everyone,
"She looks just like me!"

She looked nothing
like him—
nothing at all—
Dad was as dark as
chocolate and more
than six-feet tall!

Dad called her his angel.
He called her his dove.

He rocked her for
hours and sang
songs of love.

Dad gave her
hugs,
he showered her
with love.
He called Christine
his gift from above.

They stared in
amazement
at what they'd created.

Mom gave God all
praise—she was oh so
elated!

Dad prayed for
long life, for
grace, and for
peace.
He smiled at
Christine as she
fell fast asleep.

"Good night,
sweetheart. I'm
glad you're
resting."
Then Mom told
Dad, "She truly
is a blessing!"

All of a sudden,
our family grew.
It seemed like each
year there came
someone new.

First she had a
brother. Then
Mom had many
others. Christine's new
plea was, "Oh no, not
another!"

It soon became clear
that God had a plan.
The size of her family
was in His hand.

With her arms opened
wide, she welcomed
each sibling. Christine
was kind and warm, and
always forgiving.

She never
imagined the role
she would play in
the life of her
family until her
dying day.

Honor Roll
Ethel Twin
Naomi Jones
William Walter James Henry
Brittany Lane Nyoka Jones
Debora Darlene Calvin James
Theo Wood Annette Artelia
Devin Christopher
Phil Cleophas
Christine Townes
Vickie T. Amber Stephanie
Alvin Talley Sonya Lane
Jamie Moore Gregory T.
Kristen De'Carol Theo Cooper
Jared Townes Tabatha Artelia
Jay Jay Calvin Brea Brock
Phil Jamison Fahtima Townes
Jeremy Jewell Anita Townes
Mildred Bea

Christine was so
special and always
so helpful.

She was smart, gracious,
prudent, and an Honor
Roll student.

She was a big sister who
cared; she was always
there.

She fed us, she
cleaned us, she
combed my long
hair.

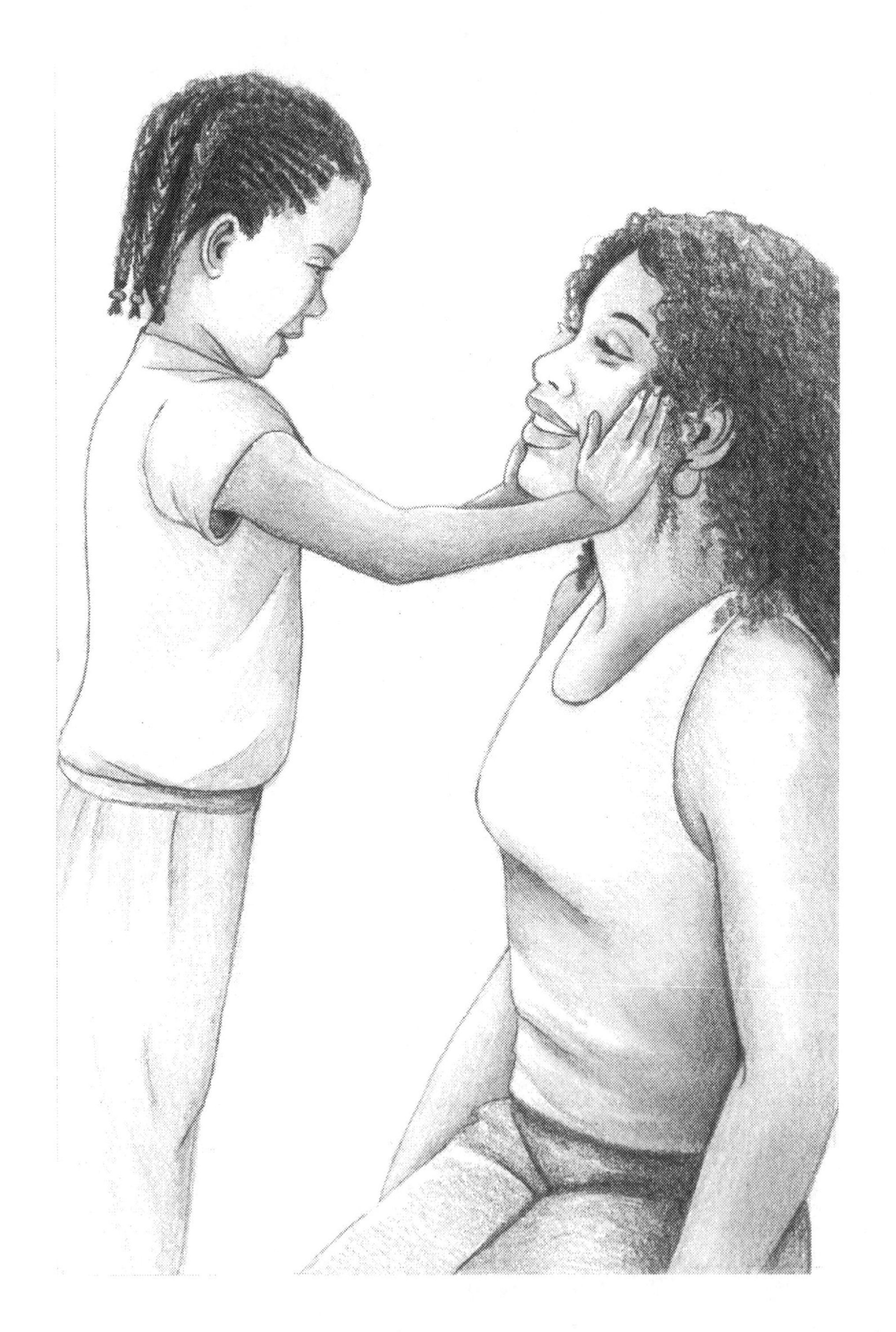

I looked up to my
sister.
She knew
everything!
I wanted to be just
like my Christine....

One day as we worked
on Aunt Lillie's farm,
Christine was shocked
as I sang her a song.

"Your voice is so
beautiful, you really can
sing!"
And I was discovered
by my sister Christine.

She helped with
our homework.
She taught us the
rules.
And always
encouraged us to
be good at school.

Just like a mother,
she gave us her
time,
cleaning and
washing. She even
spanked us
sometimes.

That was okay,
because we knew
one thing:
we'd love her
forever—our darling
Christine.

HURRAY! CHRISTINE –
Our Queen

Christine was honored
one special day.
Her friends were all
clapping and shouting,
"HURRAY!"
An Honor Roll student
and Homecoming Queen!
We were all so proud of
our sister
Christine.

As Christine got older
and became a big girl,
she went off to college
into a new world.
Things were so
different without her at
home. We were all so
forlorn. We felt so alone.

Christine's
Purpose-
Driven
Life

Mom reminded us that
our sadness wouldn't
last. That life had
seasons and this one,
too, would pass.

"Someday you'll grow
up and fulfill your life's
dreams, and discover
your purpose
just like our Christine."

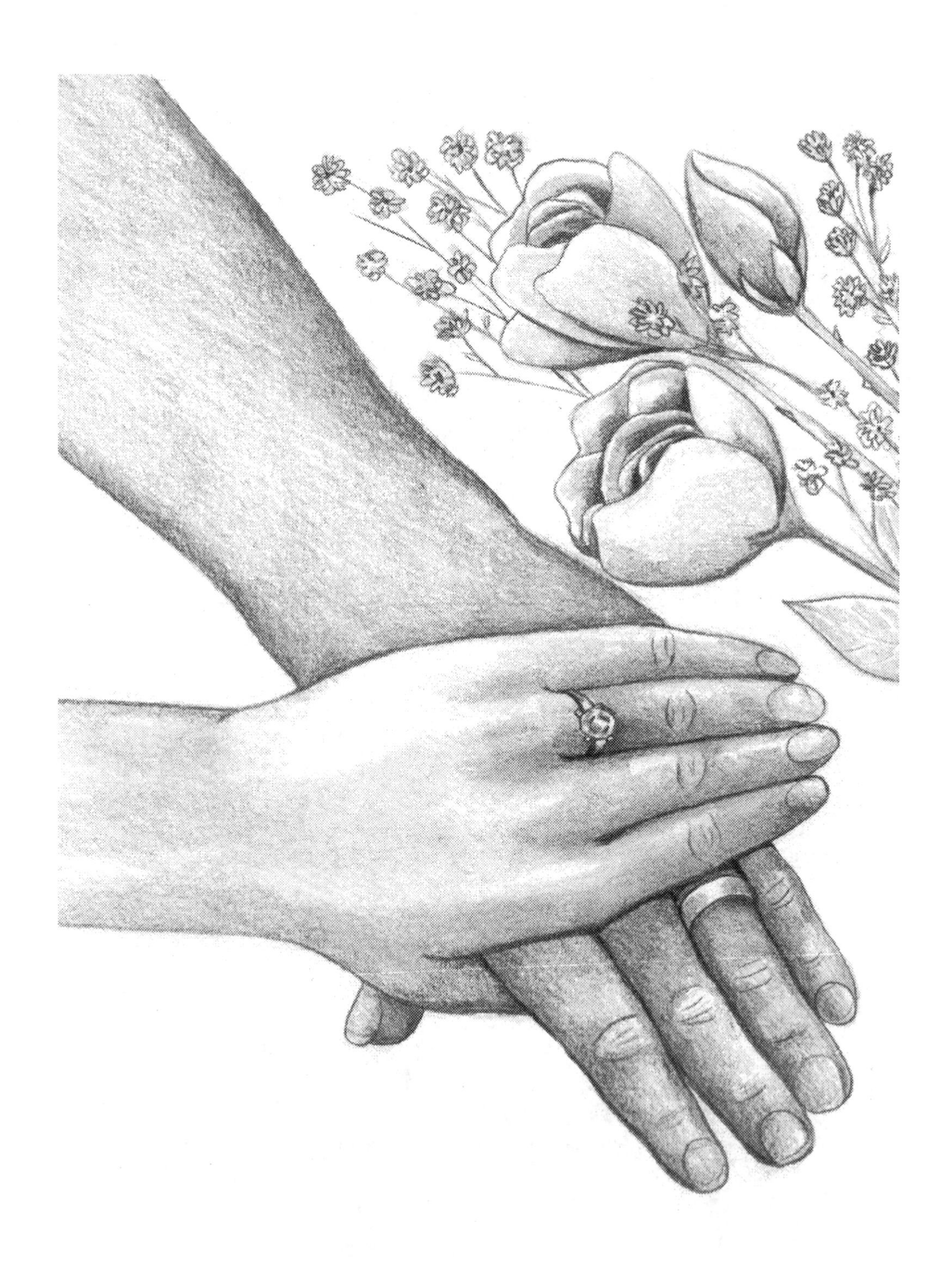

Mama's cute little girl
and Daddy's little
dove was all grown up.
She had fallen in love.

He captured her heart
and brought her a ring,
and then he married our
precious Christine.

Our family kept growing.
It grew and grew.... We
had a generation old
and a generation new.

Mama, Grandma, and
Sonya knew that
Christine loved her
family through and
through.

EMERGENCY
ENTRANCE

Everything was beautiful,
until that awful day.
That August afternoon
she almost slept away.

The doctors gave her
medicine and said, "Ya'll
keep the faith." We all
kneeled down beside
her and began to pray.

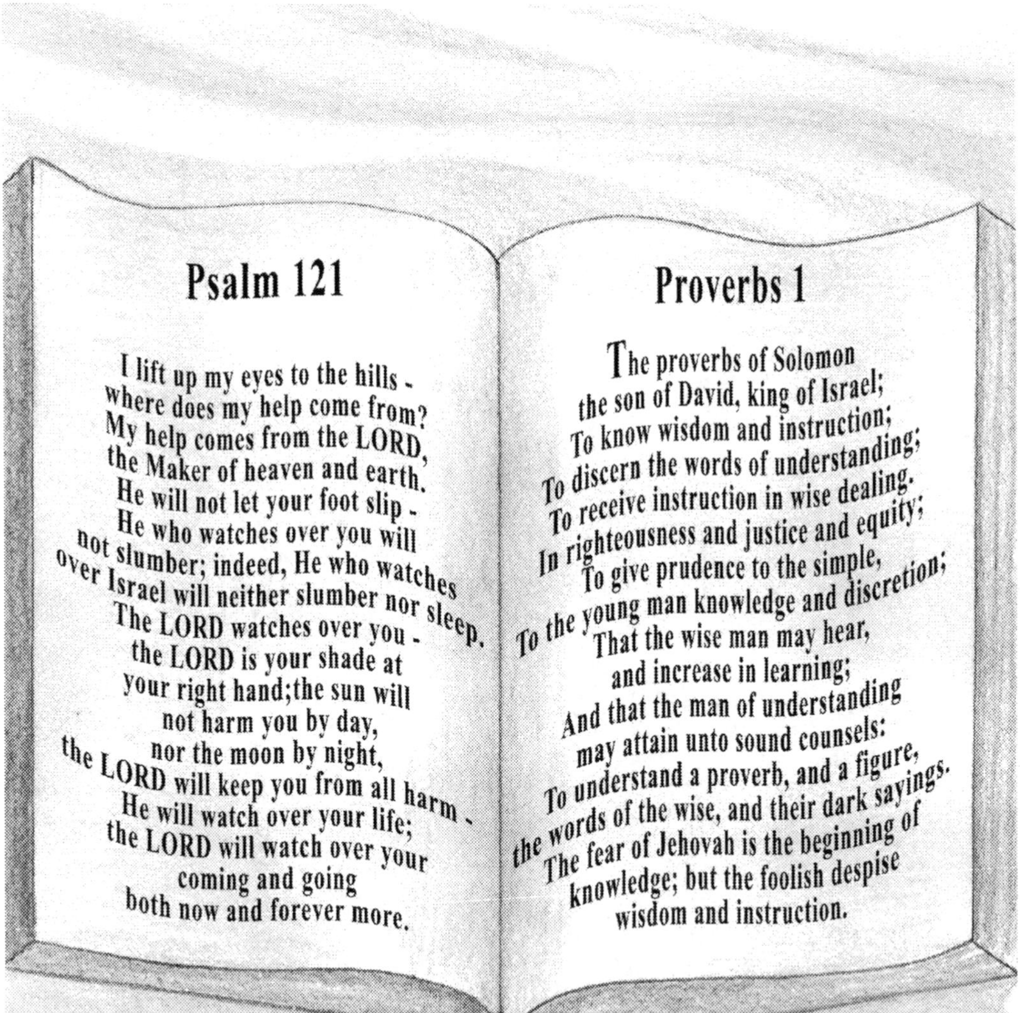

Psalm 121

I lift up my eyes to the hills -
where does my help come from?
My help comes from the LORD,
the Maker of heaven and earth.
He will not let your foot slip -
He who watches over you will
not slumber; indeed, He who watches
over Israel will neither slumber nor sleep.
The LORD watches over you -
the LORD is your shade at
your right hand;the sun will
not harm you by day,
nor the moon by night,
the LORD will keep you from all harm -
He will watch over your life;
the LORD will watch over your
coming and going
both now and forever more.

Proverbs 1

The proverbs of Solomon
the son of David, king of Israel;
To know wisdom and instruction;
To discern the words of understanding;
To receive instruction in wise dealing,
In righteousness and justice and equity;
To give prudence to the simple,
To the young man knowledge and discretion;
That the wise man may hear,
and increase in learning;
And that the man of understanding
may attain unto sound counsels:
To understand a proverb, and a figure,
the words of the wise, and their dark sayings.
The fear of Jehovah is the beginning of
knowledge; but the foolish despise
wisdom and instruction.

I kept believing,
never doubting that she
would be just fine.
I whispered Psalms and
Proverbs to feed her
mind.

It was just as I had
expected; it was no surprise!
Our beloved Christine
opened up her eyes.

Nursing
Home

Many years passed. Christine was not the same. The person I had looked up to no longer knew my name.

She pressed on
for Mimi, who
gave her loving
care.
She was a daughter oh
so special—she was
always there.

WORLD'S GREATEST
DAUGHTER
AWARDED TO
Mia Taylor

If this were a test
for the whole world to
see that she loved her
mom unconditional-
ly, she'd win an award,
she'd be on TV, and the
world would applaud
her daughter Mimi.

Sometimes this life's
journey is painful
indeed.
There will be happiness
and sorrow and there
will be times of need.

You'll never know which
one will come next.
So live your life in love
and not in regret.

Sisters
are
Forever
Christine
&
Carolyn

Christine will
always live in my
mind and in my
heart.
Though I cannot
see her, our love will
never part.

I came up with a
great idea.
I dreamed it late
one night.

It was something
very special to
celebrate her life.

Angel
KIND
BEST
SISTER
Good
Friend

We paraded down
Main Street.
We sang fun songs
and cheers.
We reminded
everyone present
that an angel had
once lived here.

Angel
BEST SISTER
KIND
Friend
Wonderful Christine
LOYAL
Good Friend

We held signs and
banners expressing
words of love
To Mama's
little queen
and Daddy's
little dove.

There was no
doubt, everyone
knew: she was held
in high esteem. They
walked away remember-
ing, there was "Nothing
Like Christine."

Remembering
the Way
We Were...

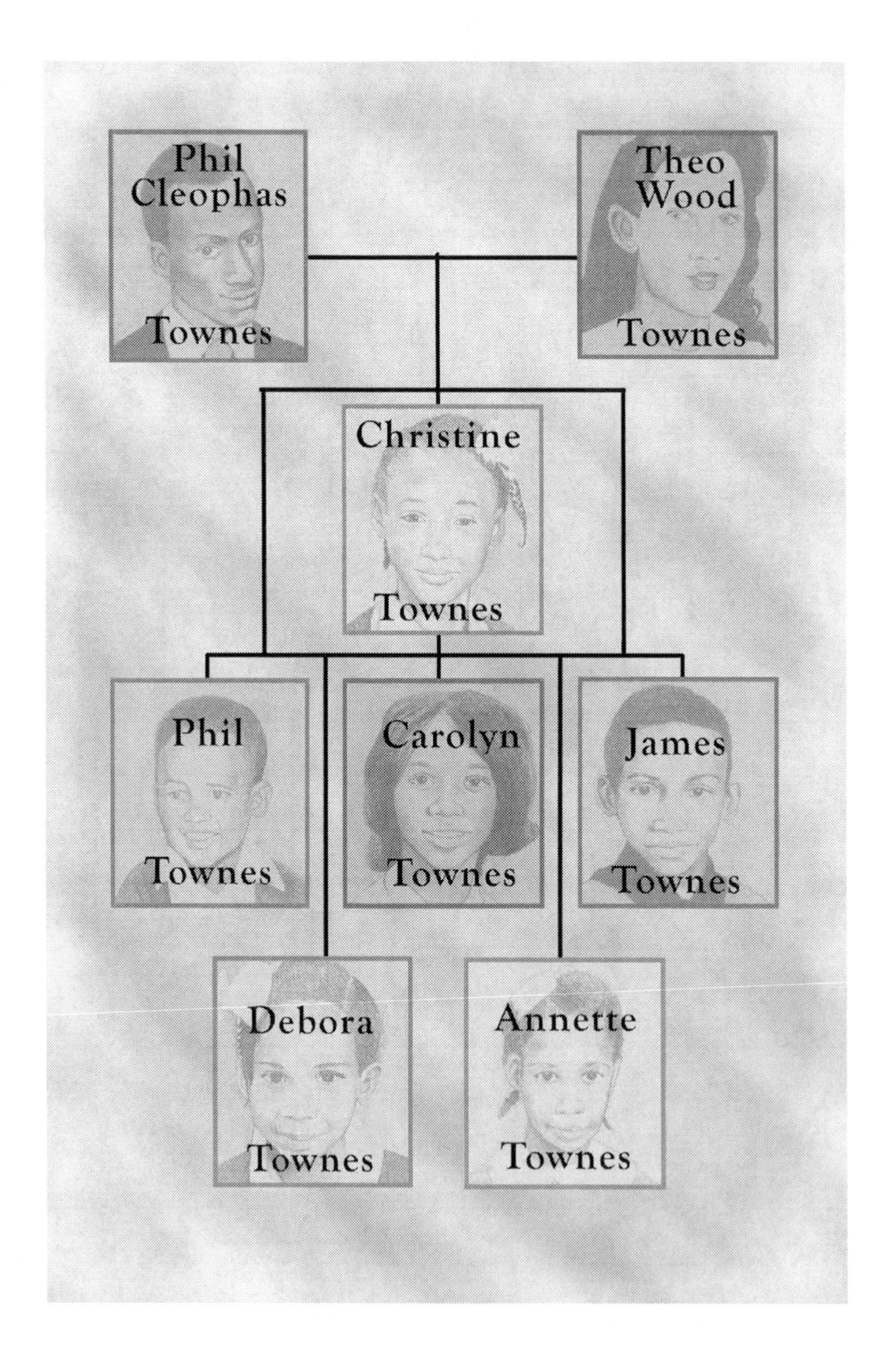
Phil
Cleophas
Townes
Theo
Wood
Townes
Christine
Townes
Phil
Townes
Carolyn
Townes
James
Townes
Debora
Townes
Annette
Townes

She Looked

Nothing Like

Sonya Taylor-Lane   Christine Townes-Taylor   Mia Denise Taylor

Christine

Special Thanks to:

Kristen DeCarol Townes

Front-Cover Model

Trinity Bryant

Model for Little Christine

Paul Richards

Model for Father

Annette Townes-Steele,

Family Photos

Wayne & Brenda Richards

Home Settings, Props, and Background

About the Author

Carolyn Townes-Richards

Is a native of Warrenton, North Carolina, and resides in New York. She is a graduate of, respectively, the College of New Rochelle, Queens College, and Barber-Scotia College. Townes-Richards is a Principal in the Hempstead School District.

Townes-Richards is also the author of Living Through Literature with Aunt CURLY'S Collection of children's books, which includes the titles:

Red on Tuesday,
At last Sonya's in the Right Lane,
and
I Promise You, Mama.

An active member of the ASCAP Writers Association, Townes-Richards has published songs for PolyGram Recording Company. She has received platinum-album status (1,000,000) for her vocal participation on the Tri-Star Movie soundtrack entitled *Breakin' II Is Electric Boogaloo.*